Holy, Hormonal, and Holding On

Finding Grace, Grit, and God in the Middle of the Midlife: Real Talk for Women of Faith Navigating Midlife, Menopause, and God's Timing

Diane Ferreira

Vale & Vine Press

Published by Vale & Vine Press, Cromwell, Connecticut

ISBN: 979-8-9993872-6-4

Library of Congress Control Number: 2025943120

Cover Design: Vale & Vine Press Interior Design: Diane Ferreira

Printed in the United States of America

Dedication

To every woman who's ever cried in the bathroom, laughed in the middle of chaos, and prayed her way through a hot flash: this book is for you.

You are seen, you are strong, and you are never alone.

Acknowledgments

To my family, thank you for letting me write about our chaos with grace and good humor.

To my friends who showed up in the middle of my mess and reminded me I still had a message, this book carries your fingerprints.

To every reader walking through the wild ride of midlife: thank you for trusting me with your time and your heart. We're holding on together.

And all the glory goes to God, the One who held me steady through my hardest days and reminded me that faith and a good sense of humor can carry you through just about anything.

Contents

Introduction

If you picked up this book hoping for a twelve-step plan to glide through midlife with glowing skin, uninterrupted sleep, and a perfectly calm spirit... bless your heart. You might want to put it down now. This isn't that.

This is the book for the woman who's holding a Bible in one hand and a heating pad in the other. The one who can quote Scripture and side-eye at the same time. The one who's wondering if her hormones are holy, her kids are okay, and her calling is still valid even if her knees pop louder than her praise music.

Midlife is weird. It's wonderful. It's wild. And it's often way louder and lonelier than we expected.

But it's also holy.

In these pages, we'll laugh (because if we don't, we'll cry), we'll dig into the Word, and we'll talk honestly about what it means to be a woman navigating spiritual purpose, shifting hormones, and sagging body parts...all while trying not to curse in traffic.

Each chapter is a midlife moment; full ofhumor, honesty, and hard-earned wisdom. They're bite-sized, but Spirit-filled. You'll find scripture, journal prompts, and truth bombs designed to remind youthat you are not crazy, you are not alone, and you are absolutely still called.

This isn't a "fix it" manual. It's a "me too" message. A love letter from one midlife woman to another, saying: You are seen. You are still in your season. And God is not done with you yet.

So, take a deep breath, grab a snack, and come on in. Holy, hormonal, and holding on? You're in good company.

SECTION 1: The Body Ain't What It Used to Be... and Neither Is My Patience

Chapter 1
Hot Flashes & Holiness
When the fire of the Spirit meets the fire in your armpits.

Let me go ahead and confess this now: I love Jesus with my whole heart, but when my internal thermostat decides to hit 450 degrees at 2:17am, I do question my salvation just a little bit. That bedside fan becomes my best friend, my washcloth becomes a ministry tool, and I'm rebuking the enemy and my own estrogen in the same breath.

Holy and hormonal? Yes, we're doing both.

There was a time when I thought "refining fire" was just a nice Bible metaphor. These days, I feel like I am the fire. Not in a glamorous, confident way, but in the sense that my body is breaking out in heat-waves like I'm trapped in a sauna I never signed up for. And the timing? Impeccable. These moments show up like uninvited guests, suddenly, awkwardly, and right when I'm trying to have a peaceful moment with God.

One minute I'm leading Bible study in a cute cardigan. The next, I'm discreetly peeling it off and hoping no one notices the sheen forming on my forehead. My glasses fog up. My upper lip starts to shine. And someone in the front row thinks I'm crying under the anointing. Not quite. That's sweat, not tears.

But here's what I've learned: being hormonal doesn't disqualify you from being holy. I'm still called, still anointed, even when I'm managing symptoms that feel inconvenient or uncomfortable. God doesn't retract your purpose just because your body is changing. If anything, He draws nearer with more grace.

Sarah's story didn't begin in her youth. Her calling came later. And maybe, just maybe, we're stepping into our most significant seasons right here in the middle of all this.

Because this isn't just about hot flashes. This is about the invisible layers of pressure and identity crisis that come with it. The shame that tries to creep in when your body won't cooperate the way it used to. The moments where your confidence slips out the door right alongside your memory and your waistline.

It's real. And it's painful. And it doesn't mean you're weak. It means you're walking through fire and still choosing to show up for your life.

I've had mornings where I cried getting dressed, not because anything tragic happened, but because nothing fit right and I didn't recognize the woman in the mirror. And I've had nights where I lay in bed wide awake, drenched in sweat, wondering if I was losing my mind or just my hormones. But here's the truth: even when I feel broken, I'm still whole in Him.

This is where the deeper work begins. God is not just helping us survive this season. He's sanctifying it. He's using every single interruption and inconvenience to deepen our trust and refine our faith. And He's not waiting for us to be "back to normal" before He meets us in it.

So, if you're waking up in the middle of the night feeling overwhelmed by heat or change, you're not alone. You're just adjusting to a new season. One filled with wisdom, deeper perspective, and strength you didn't know you had. You're not the same woman you were ten years ago. And that's a good thing.

Keep your fan close, wipe your brow, and keep pressing forward. Even when it's not comfortable, it's still sacred.

Biblical Heat: Real Fires, Real Faith

You know who else had heat? Shadrach, Meshach, and Abednego. Literal fire. And what did they say? *"Even if He doesn't rescue us, we will not bow."* That kind of resolve is a whole different level. They were in a physical furnace and didn't even smell like smoke when they came out (Daniel 3:27).

Meanwhile, I go through one hot flash and I'm ready to throw a whole fit and cancel my plans.

But their story gives me hope. Because the same God who stood in the fire with them is standing with you in this heat wave of a season. And if He can preserve them through a furnace turned up seven times hotter, He can handle your menopause.

And don't overlook Elijah either. One of the greatest prophets in the Bible, he called down fire from heaven but still ended up under a tree, exhausted, hormonal (okay, maybe not *technically*), and asking God to take him out (1 Kings 19:4).

And what did God do? He didn't rebuke him. He sent an angel with food and rest. That's our God…He understands the crash after the calling. Never underestimate the power of a snack and a nap!

Word Drop:

Your weakness doesn't cancel your witness. *(See 2 Corinthians 12:9)*

This season might feel like it's stripping things away, but it's also making room. Room to slow down. Room to dig deeper. Room to finally stop pretending that you've got it all together.

So next time you're peeling off that cardigan in public or crying over nothing in your car, just remember, you're not unraveling. You're being redefined.

You're still chosen. Still useful. Still holy. Even if your deodorant is working overtime.

Midlife isn't a detour. It's the divine rerouting of a deeper, more rooted woman.

A woman who isn't trying to go back; she's learning to go boldly forward.

Isaiah 43:2: "When you walk through the fire, you will not be burned…"

Midlife Moment: Journal Prompts

1. What has been the most surprising (or ridiculous) part of experiencing menopause or perimenopause?

2. How have your spiritual practices had to adapt during this season?

3. What's one way you've seen God's grace in the middle of hormonal chaos?

4. Where do you need to give yourself more compassion for what your body is navigating?

5. How can you bring more humor and lightness into the heaviness of this season?

Chapter 2

I Need a Nap and a Word from the Lord

Because being tired is now a spiritual gift.

I never knew exhaustion could feel like a full-time job until midlife hit. This isn't the kind of tired that a power nap or a caramel macchiato can fix. This is "I just blinked too hard and almost fell asleep in the prayer circle" kind of tired.

It sneaks up on you. One minute, you're killing it at life…leading Bible study, cooking dinner, folding laundry while quoting Scripture. And the next, you're wondering if you can cancel everything just to lie in bed and stare at the ceiling.

You used to run on coffee and conviction. Now you run on Jesus and joint supplements.

And what makes it worse is the guilt. Oh, the guilt. You feel like you should be able to push through. Everyone else looks like they're handling life just fine. But there you are, counting down to bedtime at 3:17 in the afternoon.

I've had moments where I whispered to God, "I love You, but if You could just let me take a nap first, I'll be back to finish this intercession later." And I swear He chuckled. Not in a judgmental way. In that knowing, gracious, "I got you, girl" way.

Because guess what? God does not shame us for needing rest. He actually commanded it.

Even superheroes need a Sabbath.

Sabbath was His idea, not ours. And Jesus Himself took breaks. Not just naps in boats (although that was iconic) but pauses in places of weariness where ministry still found Him.

And speaking of tired and divine timing...Jesus had a moment too.

Let's talk about that well in John 4.

A Tired Savior, A Divine Appointment

Jesus, fully divine and fully human, was walking through Samaria when He sat down at the well because He was **tired**. That's what the Bible says. Not "strategically preparing for a miraculous encounter"... He sat down because He was worn out. And from that place of physical weariness, He ministered to a woman who desperately needed to be seen.

She came to the well carrying shame and thirst and found the Living Water sitting there, catching His breath.

"So Jesus, tired from His journey, was just sitting by the well." —**John 4:6 (NASB)**

No crowds. No music. No perfect setup. Just a tired Savior, a thirsty woman, and a moment that changed her life.

Don't miss that: God moves even when you feel like you've got nothing left.

You don't have to be energized, polished, or full of pep to be powerful. Sometimes, your greatest ministry moments come when you're the most human—tired, honest, and willing to sit still.

Word Drop

Your rest doesn't cancel your calling.It creates space for a divine encounter. (See John 4:6–26)

Some days, the most spiritual thing you can do is say "no," put your feet up, and let the Lord minister to you through a fuzzy blanket and a 30-minute doze.

I used to feel guilty for wanting rest. Now I see it as stewardship. I can't pour into others from an empty cup, or worse, from a cracked one held together with caffeine and tears.

There's a sacredness in slowing down. A holiness in taking off the cape. Because when you rest, you're saying, "God, I trust You to hold it all while I recharge." That's faith.

And it's not just physical. Mental rest matters, too.

I don't know who needs to hear this, but you are not obligated to respond to every text, solve every problem, or attend every invitation. Sometimes the most anointed answer you can give is "not today."

So go ahead. Rest when you need to. Cry if you have to. Cancel the non-essentials. And let the Lord be your strength when you feel like you're running on empty.

Because some days, the most faithful thing you can do is crawl under the covers, whisper "Jesus," and trust that He's not going to love you any less for choosing the nap over the noise.

"In peace I will lie down and sleep, for you alone, Lord, make me dwell in safety." —**Psalm 4:8 (NASB)**

Midlife Moment: Journal Prompts

1. Where in your life are you feeling the most tired right now?

2. What are your beliefs about rest and productivity?

3. How can you build more intentional rest into your spiritual rhythms?

4. Where do you feel pressure to perform instead of pause?

5. What would it look like to let God meet you in your weariness, not after it?

Chapter 3
The Mirror is Lying, but Jesus Doesn't
Because some days the only thing growing fast is your chin hair.

Let's talk about mirrors. Those lying, fluorescent-lit funhouse traps. You walk by and do a double-take because...who is that woman? And why does she look slightly annoyed, deeply tired, and vaguely suspicious of her own reflection?

Welcome to midlife, where your eyebrows thin but your mustache is thriving. Where your jeans fit on Monday and betray you by Friday. Where gravity isn't just a theory, it's a lifestyle.

You used to get ready for the day by slapping on some mascara and lip gloss. Now it's a full-blown tactical mission. Concealer, creams, tweezers, readers... possibly a pep talk. You don't get dressed anymore, you assemble yourself like a spiritual IKEA project. Some assembly always required.

And yet, in the middle of all that absurdity, something sacred is happening.

Because as funny and frustrating as it is to watch your face morph and your metabolism take a nap, there's a different kind of beauty showing up. One that has nothing to do with wrinkle creams or waistlines. One that's got depth and laugh lines and eyes that have seen too much to take nonsense seriously.

You've earned every freckle. Every line. Every soft spot that used to be firm. Your body might not look the same, but it's carried babies, buried pain, fed people, and walked through fire. It's done holy work.

So yeah, we're gonna joke about the stray hairs and saggy bits. We're gonna laugh at the rogue eyebrows and the sudden need for orthopedic shoes. But let's not forget, this body, this face, this life?

It's still worthy. Still beautiful. Still full of glory.

Even if the only thing getting compressed these days is your patience.

When the Word Becomes Your Mirror

But let's go deeper for a minute.

Because the real problem isn't the mirror... it's what we believe when we look into it.

We start measuring ourselves against some old version of who we were, or some made-up version of who we think we should be. We compare ourselves to Instagram filters and women who probably haven't blinked since 2017 because Botox took their facial expressions hostage.

And we forget that Scripture already told us who we are.

"You are altogether lovely, my darling, and no blemish is in you.." —**Song of Solomon 4:7**

That verse isn't about perfection. It's about perception. When God looks at you, He sees the full picture... not just your face, but your faith. Not just your body, but your becoming.

The mirror may highlight your wrinkles. But the Word highlights your worth.

So, the next time you find yourself staring at your reflection with frustration, remind yourself: this is the face of a woman who has survived every single bad day. She's kept the faith when she didn't feel cute. She's prayed with puffy eyes and praised with stretch marks.

And God has never flinched when looking at her.

In fact, He delights in you. Right now. Not "once you get your glow back." Not "when you've dropped the weight or found the right serum." Now. As you are.

Word Drop

Your reflection is not a rejection. It's a revelation.*(See James 1:23–25)*

James says that when we look into the Word and walk away forgetting what we saw, it's like looking into a mirror and doing nothing about it.

But honey, you're doing something every single day... you're showing up. You're trusting God. You're choosing grace.

And that's what makes you radiant. That, my friend, is the glow that can't be filtered.

"They who looked to Him were radiant, and their faces will never be ashamed." —**Psalm 34:6** (some versions have verse 5).

Midlife Moment: Journal Prompts

1. What do you see when you look in the mirror lately?

2. How do you speak to yourself about your aging body?

3. Where have you seen beauty show up in unexpected places?

4. What parts of your appearance have become sources of insecurity?

5. What truths do you want to start speaking over your reflection?

Chapter 4

Lord, Heal My Knees and My Attitude

Joint pain, prayer, and petty thoughts—an honest testimony.

I used to drop to my knees in prayer. Now I lower myself down like I'm disarming a bomb. One wrong move and there's a popping noise followed by a thirty-second recovery.

Let's be real. These knees have been through it.

There was a time I could squat to clean under the couch, pop back up, and keep it moving. Now, if something rolls under there, it might as well be gone forever. "Out of sight, out of sanctification."

Midlife has brought a beautiful collection of surprises: stiffness, creaking joints, and the humbling realization that your bones can predict the weather more accurately than your local meteorologist.

But it's not just the knees, is it?

My attitude has taken a few hits, too. Patience is shorter. The filter between my thoughts and my mouth? She's on sabbatical. Things that I used to let slide now bring out a level of side-eye that requires prayer and possibly a time-out.

I've found myself praying not just for healing in my body, but in my mindset. Because physical pain has a way of sharpening emotional edges. You're tired. You're sore. And suddenly, the lady who parked too close at the grocery store becomes the reason you're rebuking everything and everyone.

The connection between body and spirit is real.

> *"A tranquil heart is life to the body, but envy is rottenness to the bones."* —**Proverbs 14:30**

Scripture doesn't separate our physical from our emotional, it sees the whole person. And let me tell you, some days I'm whole, alright... wholly annoyed, wholly tired, wholly in need of a Holy Spirit chiropractor.

And yet, God meets me in the middle of all of it.

Wholeness Starts With the Question

There's a beautiful scene in John 5 where Yeshua (Jesus in Hebrew) encounters a man at the Pool of Bethesda. This man had been lying there, disabled for thirty-eight years. When Jesus sees him, He asks, "Do you want to get well?"

Not "What's wrong with you?" Not "Why haven't you tried harder?" He just asks, "Do you want to be made whole?"

"Seeing him lying there and knowing he had been that way a long time, Yeshua said to him, 'Do you want to get well?'" —**John 5:6**

Some days, I feel like that man. Not in the exact same situation, but in the emotional sense of being worn down by years of spiritual fatigue and physical frustration. I don't always want a pep talk. I want permission to be honest with God about how I feel.

And He gives it.

When I whisper, "Lord, I'm tired of hurting," He doesn't shame me. He sits beside me at the pool of my pain and gently reminds me: wholeness is still on the table.

Healing isn't just about your knees. It's about your posture, your attitude, your expectations, your willingness to believe that even in this stage of life, God can still renew what's been worn down.

So yes, I'm praying for my knees. But I'm also praying for softness in my heart. I'm asking God to help me respond with grace when I want to roll my eyes. To breathe before I snap. To choose joy before sarcasm (or at least right after it).

Because I don't want to just age, I want to mature. And that means trusting God with both the physical pain and the prickly parts of my personality.

He's not intimidated by either.

"He heals the brokenhearted and binds up their wounds." —**Psalm 147:3**

Midlife Moment: Journal Prompts

1. What physical changes have been the most challenging for you lately?

2. How has your mood or patience shifted in this season?

3. What helps you stay kind even when you're uncomfortable?

4. Where do you need healing—in your body, your attitude, or both?

5. How can you invite God into your most unfiltered, honest moments?

SECTION 2: The Mind Games Are Real

Chapter 5
I Forgot What I Came In Here For... Again
Brain fog, frustration, and finding peace in the pause.

There I was, standing in the kitchen, staring into the fridge like it held the secrets of the universe. And for the life of me, I could not remember what I came in there for. Was it the almond milk? The eggs? Was I just hungry and confused?

Who knows. I eventually just closed the fridge and walked away like it was none of my business.

Welcome to the part of midlife no one warned us about: the mental blackouts. The brain fog. The "What did I just say?" and "Where are my glasses?" (Spoiler: they're on your head). This isn't forgetfulness from being careless, this is neurological gymnastics with zero medals and a lot of frustration.

And it's not just inconvenient. It's disorienting.

For women who've always prided themselves on managing households, jobs, schedules, Bible studies, and birthdays...this can feel like failure. Like maybe you're not as sharp, not as useful, not as needed.

But let me say this loud and clear: **you are not broken. You're just in transition.**

Your brain is still powerful. Your wisdom is still valid. And your worth? Untouchable.

"For God is not a God of confusion, but shalom."
—1 Corinthians 14:33

Yes, things might be foggy right now. Yes, you might start a sentence and finish it three days later. But God is still in it. Even when your thoughts are scattered, His presence is steady.

When the Fog Hits Deeper

I used to think brain fog was just a quirky little side effect of aging. But after my stroke at 53, I learned that sometimes, the fog comes from something much deeper.

At the time, I was doing it all: fostering a child, managing a house full of people, chickens and goats and two dogs, balancing ministry and motherhood like a well-decorated circus act. And then, in a blink, everything stopped.

My body shut down. And my mind went with it.

Recovery came slow. And with it came a sense of mental fuzziness I wasn't prepared for. I'd forget names, dates, even words. I'd start tasks and abandon them halfway through because my brain just wouldn't cooperate.

I even had to stop blogging for a year because I couldn't organize my thoughts.

And let me tell you, when your intellect has been your security blanket, watching it slip through your fingers feels terrifying.

I was afraid to admit it. Afraid people would think I wasn't capable anymore. Afraid that maybe God was done using me because I couldn't "think straight" all the time.

But that's when the Lord reminded me: **He doesn't require perfection. He requires surrender.**

> *"Trust in Adonai with all your heart, lean not on your own understanding. In all your ways acknowledge Him, and He will make your paths straight."* **—Proverbs 3:5–6**

That passage hit different in the fog. I wasn't leaning on my understanding, because there wasn't much of it some days. I was clinging to Him, trusting that He could still lead me even when I couldn't find my car keys.

And you know what? He did.

He used my brain fog to slow me down. To silence the hustle. To remind me that my value doesn't come from how productive or mentally sharp I am, it comes from the fact that I am His.

So now, when I wander into a room and forget why I'm there, I don't panic. I pause. I laugh. I remind myself that forgetfulness isn't failure...it's a nudge to slow down, breathe deep, and maybe grab a snack while I figure it out.

Midlife doesn't mean your mind is slipping. It means your priorities are shifting. And maybe, just maybe, it's time to stop trying to remember everything...and start remembering the *One* who holds everything together.

Even you.

Word Drop:

When your thoughts feel tangled and your memory feels like a game of hide-and-seek, don't let shame creep in. You are not less spiritual because your brain needs a breather. God's grace covers brain fog too.

> *"You will keep in perfect peace one whose mind is steadfast, because he trusts in You."* —**Isaiah 26:3**

Let that be your anchor when your thoughts scatter like confetti at a toddler's birthday party. Peace is not about perfection. It's about presence...His presence.

Midlife Moment: Journal Prompts

1. When do you most notice brain fog showing up in your life?

2. How do you respond to moments of forgetfulness?

3. What pressures do you feel to always have it together?

4. Where can you offer yourself more grace this week?

5. How can you invite God into your moments of mental over-whelm?

Chapter 6
Mood Swings and Ministry
How to cry, pitch a fit, and still serve faithfully.

There are days I wake up ready to cast out demons and take on the world. And then by 2:17pm, I'm weeping into a bag of pretzels because someone didn't text me back.

Welcome to ministry in midlife, where your heart is full of calling but your hormones are playing dodgeball with your sanity.

We don't talk about this enough. That weird, emotional whiplash that comes when you're trying to serve others while silently wondering if you're the one who needs an altar call. One minute you're in full intercessory flow, praying like Elijah. The next, you're glaring at your husband because he chews too loud.

It's not a lack of faith. It's a **very real mix** of spiritual burden and physical reality.

Our emotions are God-given, but when they spike and drop like a bad day at the stock market, it gets hard to tell what's Holy Spirit and what's hot flash. That's why midlife ministry takes more than anointing oil. It takes *honesty*.

And if no one else is going to say it, I will: **serving others while navigating mood swings is a whole ministry in itself.**

Ministry, Martha, and Meltdowns

There's a powerful scene in the Gospels where Yeshua encounters Martha. She's overwhelmed, under-appreciated, and sis is definitely having a moment.

> *"Martha, Martha," Yeshua answered, "you are anxious and bothered about many things; but only one thing is necessary. For Miriam has chosen the good part, which will not be taken away from her."*
> —**Luke 10:41–42**

That's the thing. Ministry doesn't mean we have to be emotionally flawless. It means we have to choose what matters most even when everything in us wants to spiral.

We can serve, but we must also sit. We can pour out, but not at the expense of our peace. And when our moods feel louder than our message, it's time to hit pause and realign with the One who sees through the chaos and speaks peace.

God doesn't shame us for our emotions. He doesn't flinch when we break down over dinner prep or sob on the bathroom floor. He created us with depth, and that includes days where we're one broken nail away from falling apart.

You are not failing because you feel deeply. You are not disqualified because your emotions show up in full color.

You are still called. Still chosen. Still equipped to serve.

> *"Adonai is near to the brokenhearted and saves those crushed in spirit." —Psalm 34:19*

Even when you feel like a holy hot mess, He's near.

So, if you find yourself sobbing between worship sets or internally snapping during a women's conference, take heart. You're not alone.

Your ministry isn't less valid because you're navigating emotions...it's more authentic because you are.

Word Drop:

Your emotional waves do not disqualify you from your divine assignment. They just remind you that you're human; one deeply loved, deeply called human.

> *"He gives strength to the weary, and to one without vigor He adds might."—Isaiah 40:29*

Let that soak in the next time your mascara and your mood give up at the same time. God is not alarmed by your mood swings, He's present in them.

"Be still and know that I am God." —**Psalm 46:11**

Midlife Moment: Journal Prompts

1. What emotions have felt the strongest lately?

2. How do you typically handle emotional ups and downs?

3. Where do you feel pressure to be "okay" even when you're not?

4. What does it look like to give yourself grace in emotional moments?

5. How can you invite God into your mood swings and ministry?

Chapter 7
The Comparison Trap Hits Different at 50+

She's thriving. You're here just trying not to forget your phone number.

Can we be real for a minute?

There's nothing like scrolling through social media after a long day, in your bathrobe, hair in a half-bun, one sock on, and boom... there she is.

Some stranger in a wide-brim hat sipping oat milk lattes with perfect lighting and a caption that reads, "Just feeling so blessed in this season of growth."

Meanwhile, you're just trying not to burn the frozen pizza and wondering if "season of growth" refers to your waistline.

Comparison isn't new. We've been doing it since Eve and that fruit. But something about midlife makes it cut deeper. We're not just comparing accomplishments, we're comparing timelines, energy levels, hormone balances, and the softness of our neck skin.

At this age, you start asking questions like:

- "Should I be further along?"

- "Why does she look so put together while I feel like a Pinterest fail?"

- "Am I too late to live the life I dreamed of?"

And here's the truth I had to come to grips with: **comparison will always rob you of clarity.**

"Let us walk properly as in the day—not in carousing and drunkenness, not in sexual immorality and sensuality, not in strife and envy." —Romans 13:13

Did you catch that last part? *Not in strife and envy.* Because the moment you start looking left and right, you stop walking straight ahead.

The Trap, the Truth, and the Tender Whisper

I once lost half a day spiraling because someone I knew (younger, tanner, and with tighter triceps) launched a new devotional. I was genuinely happy for her... and also wondering if I was past my prime.

But the Spirit whispered something sharp and kind: "You are not in competition with her. You are on assignment from Me."

That'll humble you real quick.

God doesn't give out gold stars for who gets there first. He honors faithfulness, not finish lines. And while you're eyeing her highlight reel, you're missing the beauty of your own behind-the-scenes obedience.

> *"For where jealousy and selfish ambition exist, there is disorder and every evil practice. But the wisdom that is from above is first pure, then peaceable, gentle, open to reason, full of mercy and good fruits, impartial, not hypocritical."*—**James 3:16–17**

That verse doesn't just convict me, it calms me. Because I don't want the disorder that comes with jealousy. I want the peace that flows from wisdom.

Word Drop:

The woman you're comparing yourself to? She's not your competition, she's your sister. And your journey still matters, even if it looks nothing like hers.

> *"A tranquil heart is life to the body, but envy is rottenness to the bones."*—**Proverbs 14:30**

You weren't made to be her. You were made to be **His**. And that is more than enough.

Let her be inspiring, not intimidating.

*"Each one must examine his own work. Then he will have pride in himself alone and not in comparison to anyone else." —***Galatians 6:4**

Midlife Moment: Journal Prompts

1. When do you notice comparison creeping in most?

2. What are some lies it tells you?

3. What truth from God's Word can you speak back to those lies?

4. How do you want to redefine success in this season?

5. Who are you when no one is watching, and how can you celebrate her more?

Chapter 8
My Timeline Is in God's Hands (and That's Kinda Annoying)
Surrendering your five-year plan...again.

If I had a dollar for every plan I made that didn't happen, I could at least afford all the supplements midlife requires.

There's something deeply humbling about watching your carefully thought-out schedule get steamrolled by divine detours. And let me tell you, God's timing? It's beautiful. It's holy. And sometimes... well, it's just plain inconvenient.

We live in a culture that says "set goals," "hustle hard," "claim your destiny." But what happens when the doors don't open? When the yeses are delayed, the growth feels stunted, and your planner is filled with empty boxes and unrealized dreams?

You start to wonder if you missed something.

But here's the truth: **you didn't miss it. You're being *meticulously led*.**

"Adonai is not slow in keeping His promise, as some consider slowness. Rather, He is being patient toward you—not wanting anyone to perish, but for all to come to repentance." —**2 Peter 3:9**

God's version of "on time" isn't the same as ours. We're thinking next quarter, He's thinking eternity.

I remember turning 50 and thinking, "This should be my harvest season." I was ready for the big stuff. The breakthroughs. The fruit. But instead, it felt like more pruning. More waiting. More of the uncomfortable in-between.

That's when I had to come face to face with the lie I'd been believing: that *delay means denial*.

It doesn't.

God's delay isn't punishment, it's preparation. And sometimes, what feels like stagnation is actually sacred space to get your heart right before the harvest.

When Delay Feels Like Denial

"He has made everything beautiful in its time."
—**Ecclesiastes 3:11**

I've clung to that verse like it's oxygen. Because if I'm honest, I've grieved over timelines that didn't pan out. Over the "should have happened by now" moments. Over the feeling that maybe I'm behind. But God keeps reminding me: you're not behind, you're just *on My time*.

And here's the kicker: His timing is always aligned with His love. He's not out to frustrate you. He's preparing you.

Sometimes the thing we're waiting on is less about the thing and more about who we're becoming while we wait.

Word Drop:

Delayed doesn't mean denied. You are not forgotten, you are being formed. And that waiting season? It's working even when you can't see it.

"Wait for Adonai. Be strong, let your heart take courage, and wait for Adonai."—**Psalm 27:14**

He's not late. He's layering every detail with care.

"Faithful is the One who calls you—and He will make it happen!"—**1 Thessalonians 5:24**

Midlife Moment: Journal Prompts

1. What dreams or plans have felt delayed in your life?

2. How have you responded to those delays emotionally and spiritually?

3. Where is God inviting you to surrender your timeline?

4. What can you celebrate about the season you're in—even if it's not what you planned?

5. How can you trust that your pace is not a problem in God's plan?

SECTION 3:
Relationships, Boundaries & Blessings

Chapter 9
When My Kids Don't Need Me, But My Dog Still Does

Empty nest, evolving roles, and letting go with grace (kinda).

There's a moment most moms don't see coming. It's not the first day of kindergarten or the driver's license test or even the college drop-off. It's that quiet Tuesday morning when you realize... no one needs you to pack a lunch.

Your house is clean-ish. Your phone isn't blowing up with "Mom, where's my—?" And suddenly, you're not in demand the way you used to be.

It's bittersweet. It's weird. And it's not exactly what you prayed for, but here it is: *an emptyish nest and a very needy bulldog.*

My dog, bless his little flat-faced soul, is living his best life. He follows me everywhere (at least until my husband gets home) like I'm the queen and he's the security detail. He demands snacks. He gives judgmental side-eyes when I don't share my yogurt. And honestly? He's a bit of a comfort. Because while the house is quieter, the love is still loud. Even if it comes with fur, slobber, and dramatic sighs.

But this season? This shift from full-on motherhood to whatever-this-is now? It stirs things up.

You start asking, "Who am I when I'm not needed all the time?""Is it okay to enjoy this freedom?""Do I still matter if no one calls me for help today?"

And the answer is yes. You do.

"Your wife will be like a fruitful vine within your house. Your children will be like olive plants around your table." **—Psalm 128:3**

That verse hits different now. Because the vine still has fruit, even when the olive plants have moved out.

Your role may be changing, but your value is not.

This is where legacy starts to grow roots. In the stillness. In the letting go. In the strange in-between where you're not driving to cheer practices or helping with homework but still praying over grown children who face battles you can't fix anymore.

Letting go is hard. But it's not the same as giving up. It's trusting that what you've planted in your kids...love, truth, resilience...is going to bloom even when you're not in the room.

"Train up a child in the way he should go, when he is old he will not turn from it." **—Proverbs 22:6**

We don't always get to see the fruit immediately. Sometimes, our job is just to keep showing up in prayer and trust that God is still parenting them even when we're not.

And let's not forget, you're still in the picture. You just might not be center stage anymore. And that's okay. Background doesn't mean backstage. It means your support is still powerful...just quieter.

Word Drop:

You didn't lose your purpose when your house got quieter. You gained space to rediscover your voice beyond everyone else's needs.

> *"Even to your old age I will be the same, until your hair is gray I will carry you. I have done it—I will bear you—I will carry you—I will deliver you."*—Isaiah 46:4

Your job may shift, but your worth is unwavering.

> *"Behold, I am doing a new thing. Now it springs forth. Do you not perceive it?"*—Isaiah 43:19

Midlife Moment: Journal Prompts

1. What emotions has the empty nest stirred up in you?

2. How has your role as a mother shifted?

3. What new opportunities or passions could this season hold?

4. Where do you still feel deeply needed and valuable?

5. How can you intentionally reconnect with yourself now?

Chapter 10
Marriage, Menopause, and Mercy

When your hormones are wild and he still chews too loud.

Let's talk marriage... post-40. You know, that sacred union that now includes arguing about the thermostat, side-eyeing each other's chewing habits, and wondering why his snoring sounds like a freight train rolling through your dreams.

I love my husband. I do. He is my best friend and is honestly the best husband in the world. But menopause has made me question that love between 2 and 4 a.m.

The truth is, midlife doesn't just change your body, it changes your rhythm. Your marriage, once built on passion and plans, now has to survive through patience, prayer, and the occasional passive-aggressive sigh.

It's not that we don't love each other. It's that we're both evolving in ways we didn't fully see coming. He's quieter now. I'm louder. He falls asleep in 3.7 seconds. I lay there, wide-eyed, having a spiritual and hormonal crisis.

And yet, even in the mess, the Lord is still working.

When Mercy Feels Louder Than Romance

"Above all, keep your love for one another constant, for 'love covers a multitude of sins.'" —**1 Peter 4:8**

Let me tell you, love has covered a multitude of mismatched socks, miscommunications, and more than one meltdown involving an empty ice cream carton. But it's also what holds us steady.

Marriage at this age is, at times, less about big romantic gestures and more about checking in. It's in the little mercies. Like him not saying a word when I cry for no reason. Or me not lighting him up for breathing too loud during a commercial break.

We need mercy for each other, but we also need mercy for ourselves.

Because I don't always respond with grace. I've slammed a few cabinet doors. Said a few sharp words. Looked at him like he was the reason the dryer shrunk my jeans. But I've also come back to the table. Apologized. Laughed. Forgiven.

"Let all bitterness and anger and wrath and clamor and slander be put away from you, with all malice. Instead, be kind to one another, compassionate, forgiving each other just as God in Messiah also

forgave you."
—Ephesians 4:31–32

Marriage is holy ground, even when it feels like holy tension. It's choosing to hold hands even when you're mad. Choosing to stay when leaving would be easier. Choosing to believe that your union still has purpose in this season.

Word Drop:

It's not about being the perfect wife, it's about being present, patient, and covered in grace. The marriage may shift, but the covenant holds.

"Two are better than one because they get a good return for their labor. For if they fall, the one will lift up his companion."—**Ecclesiastes 4:9–10**

You are not in this alone. God's in the middle of your mess and your marriage.

"Let us not lose heart in doing good, for in due time we will reap if we do not give up." —**Galatians 6:9**

Midlife Moment: Journal Prompts

1. What's been the biggest shift in your marriage during this season?

2. How can you show your spouse grace this week?

3. Where do you feel unseen or misunderstood in your relationship?

4. What small moments still make you feel connected?

5. How can you invite God into your marriage in a new way?

Chapter 11
No is a Holy Word

Setting boundaries without burning bridges ... or going to jail.

Let's start with this truth: you're allowed to say no. You're allowed to not explain it, not soften it, and not feel guilty about it. No is not a rejection, it's a revelation of your limits.

And sis, midlife teaches you your limits real quick.

You reach a point where you no longer have the time, energy, or emotional capacity to be everybody's yes-woman. That season of saying "yes" to every baby shower, potluck, and last-minute crisis? It's over. That girl is tired. And healed.

> *"But let your 'Yes' be 'Yes,' and your 'No' be 'No.'*
> *Anything more than this is from the evil one."*
> **—Matthew 5:37**

Jesus didn't waffle. He didn't say, "Well, let me pray on it for three days while I rearrange my entire life to make you feel better about my boundaries." No. He said what He meant and moved on with purpose.

You can love people deeply and still have a backbone. You can be Spirit-filled and still have spiritual boundaries. You can say "no" with grace and not lose your salvation or your social life.

I used to bend myself into holy pretzels trying to keep the peace. I'd take on too much, commit to too many things, and then lie in bed at night wondering why I was bitter, bloated, and behind on my own calling.

Midlife snapped me out of that.

This season requires clarity, not chaos. Peace, not people-pleasing.

"Seek shalom and pursue it." —**Psalm 34:15**

Peace is not just the absence of conflict, it's the presence of alignment. And if your soul is screaming "I don't want to," listen to her. She's not being dramatic. She's being discerning.

Word Drop:

Every yes costs you something. Make sure you're not paying with your peace. A no to them might just be a yes to your health, your home, or your healing.

"Do not be conformed to this world but be trans-formed by the renewing of your mind, so that you may discern what is the will of God—what is good and acceptable and perfect." —**Romans 12:2**

Boundaries are not barriers, they're bridges back to sanity.

"Fear of man proves to be a snare, but one who trusts in Adonai will be kept safe." —**Proverbs 29:25**

Midlife Moment: Journal Prompts

1. Where do you feel most drained right now?

2. What have you said yes to that needs a loving no?

3. Who respects your boundaries—and who challenges them?

4. How does saying no create space for what matters most?

5. What would your life look like if your no was as powerful as your yes?

Chapter 12

When Your Circle Gets Smaller, but Your Peace Gets Bigger

Friendships that shift and pruning that saves your soul.

Nobody warns you that friendship in your 40s and 50s comes with its own kind of drama... the *absence* of it.

One day, you're juggling brunch plans, birthday parties, and group chats with names like "Mom Squad 3.0." The next? You're sitting in your kitchen with your dog and a lukewarm cup of coffee wondering why your phone has been suspiciously silent for three days.

Here's the deal: your circle shrinking doesn't mean your value did. It just means you outgrew some rooms...and that's not always a tragedy. Sometimes it's a testimony.

"The righteous choose their friends carefully,
but the way of the wicked leads them astray."
—Proverbs 12:26

Midlife friendship hits different. You don't have time for passive-aggressive vibes, group chats that drain your spirit, or people who ghost you until they need prayer or a ride to the airport.

This isn't bitterness. It's *clarity.*

You're learning to bless people as they exit... and bless yourself as you grow.

Some relationships were seasonal. Others were spiritual training grounds. But now? You want friends who check on your soul, not just your schedule. Who clap when you win, cry when you're low, and tell you when you've got spinach in your teeth *and* pride in your heart.

> **"Iron sharpens iron—so one person sharpens another."—Proverbs 27:17**

That kind of friendship is rare. And you know what? That's okay.

Fewer people doesn't mean less love. It means you've traded noise for nourishment. You've stopped auditioning for connections that were never meant to hold your weight. And you've realized that peace is a person—*Jesus*—and sometimes He clears a room to make more space for Himself.

Word Drop:

You're not losing friends. You're gaining discernment. And sometimes peace sounds like silence.

When Pruning Makes Room for Peace

> *"He will be like a tree planted by streams of water, producing its fruit in its season. Its leaf does not wither—and in whatever he does, he succeeds."*
> **—Psalm 1:3**

Grow where you're planted...even if the garden feels a little emptier than it used to.

> *"A friend loves at all times, and a brother is born for adversity."* **—Proverbs 17:17**

Midlife Moment: Journal Prompts

1. Who are your "peace people", the ones who bring calm, not chaos?

2. Where have you felt loss in your friendships, and how have you processed it?

3. What qualities matter most to you in a friend at this stage?

4. Are there relationships you're holding onto out of guilt or history rather than growth?

5. How has your definition of friendship evolved over the years?

SECTION 4: Faith in the Flames

Chapter 13
God, I'm Too Old for This... Aren't I?

When your calling keeps growing but so does your sciatica.

There's this quiet little lie that creeps in somewhere after 50. It usually shows up when you're rubbing your knees after getting off the couch or when you forget why you walked into the room. It whispers, "You've missed your moment."

Excuse me? Who told us that purpose has an expiration date?

> *"Even in old age they will be fresh and flourishing."*
> **—Psalm 92:15**

Now look, I'm not saying I'm old. I'm just saying I make more noise getting out of bed than I used to. But while the knees may creak, the call is still clear. God didn't retire you. He's just repurposing your rhythm.

When I had my stroke, I genuinely wondered if my best years were behind me. I felt slow. I felt unsure. And I felt *old*. But here's what the Lord reminded me through all of it: you don't age out of Kingdom work. You mature into it.

We spend our youth trying to prove ourselves, trying to be seen, trying to hustle. Midlife says, "Let's do this different." With grace. With wisdom. With shoes that don't hurt.

"For the gifts and the calling of God are irrevocable." —Romans 11:29

If God called you in your 20s, He still means it in your 50s. If He whispered that dream in your heart before menopause, He's not taking it back just because your back now needs support pillows and Epsom salt.

This season isn't about chasing what used to be. It's about stewarding what still is.

You've got the oil of experience. You've got stories that can save somebody else's sanity. You've got discernment that was forged in disappointment. You're not too old, you're too seasoned to settle.

And don't let the culture fool you into thinking this is your decline. In God's economy, this could be your *launch*.

Word Drop:

It's not too late. You're not too old. And if God gave you breath this morning, He's not done using it for His glory.

"The glory of young men is their strength, and the splendor of old men is their gray hair." **—Proverbs 20:29**

Gray is glory. And wrinkles? They're just laugh lines from decades of divine encounters.

*"They will still yield fruit in old age. They will be full of sap and freshness."***—Psalm 92:15**

Midlife Moment: Journal Prompts

1. What dreams have you put on hold because of age?

2. Where have you felt God stirring something new in this season?

3. What gifts do you bring now that you didn't have ten years ago?

4. How can you encourage someone else who thinks they're "too old" to be used?

5. What would it look like to say yes to God, right now, as you are?

Chapter 14

I Love You, Lord, But I Also Need a Snack

Balancing fasting, feasting, and not fighting everybody.

Some mornings I wake up feeling all spiritual and surrendered. Ready to seek the Lord, dive into the Word, maybe even fast and pray. Then somewhere around 10:17 a.m., I'm rebuking the devil and Googling "how long until a fast still counts if I accidentally ate a cracker?"

Look, I love Jesus with my whole heart. But I also love snacks. And in this midlife season, I've learned that spiritual discipline doesn't mean ignoring your body. It means learning to listen to it through the lens of grace.

"So whether you eat or drink or whatever you do, do all to the glory of God."—**1 Corinthians 10:31**

That includes the protein shake *and* the peanut butter cups, baby.

There's this weird guilt that can creep in, especially for women of faith, around food. Like if you're not juicing celery or intermittent fasting while reciting Leviticus, you're somehow less holy. But God never called us to shame ourselves into submission.

He called us to steward these bodies with care, not cruelty.

I've fasted out of discipline. I've also fasted out of desperation. And I've broken fasts with both repentance and a chocolate chip muffin. God met me in all of it.

Because what He really wants isn't a perfect diet, it's a yielded heart.

"Then Adonai will answer and say to His people: 'Behold, I will send you the grain, the new wine and the fresh oil, and you will be satisfied with it.'"—Joel 2:19

See? Satisfaction is biblical. So is feasting. So is celebration.

It's okay to enjoy food. To nourish your body. To savor a meal with people you love without mentally calculating how to "make up for it" later. God gave us taste buds for a reason. He didn't make your joy contingent on calorie counts.

The challenge, especially now, is balance.

When hormones rage and emotions swing and comfort food calls out your name like a psalmist with a pie, how do you respond?

With honesty.

You admit when you're turning to food for comfort only God can provide. And you don't beat yourself up, you bring yourself back.

Word Drop:

The table isn't your enemy. It's a place where God meets you. You can break bread and still be whole.

> *"Yeshua said to them, 'I am the bread of life. Whoever comes to Me will never be hungry, and whoever believes in Me will never be thirsty.'"*—**John 6:35**

Sister, you're allowed to love the Lord and love lunch. Just don't let one replace the other.

> *"Taste and see how good Adonai is. Blessed is the one who takes refuge in Him."* —**Psalm 34:9**

Midlife Moment: Journal Prompts

1. What are your go-to comfort foods, and what emotions are tied to them?

2. How do you balance enjoying food with honoring your health and spirit?

3. When do you feel most tempted to feed your feelings?

4. What role does fasting (or feasting) play in your spiritual walk?

5. What would it look like to invite God into your eating habits, without guilt, but with grace?

Chapter 15
Legacy over Likes
Raising purpose instead of platform.

Somewhere along the way, culture started convincing us that impact is only real if it's public. That if it doesn't get shared, reshared, and hashtagged, it doesn't matter. That "being used by God" has to come with a microphone, a following, and a curated aesthetic.

But let me say this clearly, with love and maybe a little holy sass: **God is not checking your analytics. He's checking your obedience.**

> *"Let another praise you, and not your own*
> *mouth—a stranger, and not your own lips."*
> **—Proverbs 27:2**

The quiet things? The faithful things? The behind-the-scenes, no-one-saw-it-but-God things? That's legacy work.

You don't have to go viral to go eternal.

Legacy is built in small moments. It's when you pray for your children before they walk out the door. It's when you show up to serve with no title and no fanfare. It's when you forgive without applause. That's what echoes into the next generation, not your content calendar.

And if you're called to build a platform, praise God! Use it wisely. But don't get so caught up in who's watching that you lose sight of the One you're working for.

> *"Whatever you do, work at it from the soul, as for the Lord and not for people."*—**Colossians 3:23**

I've had moments where I wondered if I was doing enough. If what I wrote mattered. If the small room was worth the effort. But God keeps whispering, "Yes, daughter. It's not about being seen. It's about being faithful."

Purpose doesn't need a platform. It needs a posture. One that says, "Lord, use me, even if no one claps. Even if no one comments. Even if the only 'like' I get is from You."

Word Drop:

Your legacy isn't in your followers. It's in your faithfulness. And God is keeping receipts, even when no one else sees the seeds you've sown.

> *"Her children arise and bless her, her husband also praises her: 'Many daughters have excelled, but you surpass them all.'"*—**Proverbs 31:28–29**

Live for the well done... not the well-liked. #blessed

"Commit your work to Adonai and your plans will succeed." —**Proverbs 16:3**

Midlife Moment: Journal Prompts

1. Where have you felt the pull toward platform more than purpose?

2. What does "legacy" mean to you in this season?

3. Who in your life is watching your faith walk up close?

4. What seeds are you planting now that you hope will bloom later?

5. How can you shift your focus from visibility to impact?

Chapter 16
Holy, Hormonal, and Holding On

You're not just surviving this season, you're slaying it in prayer, power, and purpose.

Let's just go ahead and say it: midlife is wild.

It's holy chaos. One minute you're quoting Scripture and speaking life. The next minute you're crying in the parking lot over a Chick-fil-A order that came out wrong. You're forgetting birthdays, questioning your career, Googling weird body symptoms at midnight, and still managing to show up for people with a semi-clean shirt and a half-decent smile.

If that's not spiritual warfare with lashes on, I don't know what is.

> *"But He said to me, 'My grace is sufficient for you, for power is made perfect in weakness.'"* —2 **Corinthians 12:9**

And isn't that what this whole season is teaching us? That we can be a little undone and still be divinely appointed.

Yes, you're hormonal. Yes, you're overwhelmed. But sis, you're also anointed. You are walking, talking proof that God can still work through fluctuating emotions, forgotten passwords, and the fact that you've been wearing the same bra for three days straight.

You are holy. You are held. And you're doing better than you think.

This book wasn't written to give you a ten-step plan to fix it all. It was written to remind you that you're not alone. That you can laugh and cry and rage and pray... and God will still meet you right there in the middle of your midlife mayhem.

> *"I have set Adonai always before me. Since He is at my right hand, I will not be shaken."* —**Psalm 16:8**

You may be shaking... but you won't be shaken.

You've walked through grief and loss. You've navigated diagnoses, disappointments, and divine delays. And yet here you are...still praising. Still pressing. Still holding on.

Word Drop:

You're not just going through it. You're growing through it. Hormonal, tired, stretched thin, and still chosen.

"Adonai will accomplish that which concerns me. Your lovingkindness, Adonai, endures forever. Do not abandon the work of Your hands."—**Psalm 138:8**

He hasn't abandoned you. Not for a second.

"The path of the righteous is like the light of dawn, shining brighter and brighter until full day." —**Proverbs 4:18**

Midlife Moment: Journal Prompts

1. Where have you seen God move in your messiest moments?

2. What parts of this season feel heavy—and how are you holding on?

3. How can you give yourself more grace in this chapter?

4. What are you still believing for, even now?

5. Who can you encourage today with the reminder that midlife is still holy?

Chapter 17
Bless This Midlife Mess
Because sometimes the wheels fall off... and we keep driving anyway.

Midlife isn't always a glow-up. Sometimes it's a full-blown unraveling. Your hormones are on a rollercoaster, your sleep schedule has given up entirely, and your body makes mystery noises when you stand up.

You've got a to-do list that's never fully done, and a bathroom drawer filled with half-used products that promised miracles. (Spoiler: the under-eye cream didn't fix your soul.)

You forget names, burn dinner, and have full conversations with yourself in the Target parking lot. You misplace your keys while holding them and question if leggings count as pants more often than you'd like to admit.

And in the middle of this beautiful, chaotic circus, you're still showing up. Still loving people. Still praying. Still laughing. Still hoping. Still pushing through.

Bless this mess.

Bless the woman who forgot what she walked into the room for. Bless the coffee that got reheated three times. Bless the days that feel like a hundred little fires and the nights that come too fast.

Because here's the thing: your mess doesn't disqualify you. It doesn't make you less spiritual or less worthy. If anything, it makes you more relatable. Nobody needs another perfect Christian woman who floats around quoting Proverbs and eating kale.

We need women who are real. Who have cried in bathroom stalls and praised God with puffy eyes. Women who know how to laugh at the madness and still find God in the middle of it.

So, bless the mascara-smudged, dry-shampooed, overly-caffeinated glory of this season. Bless the chaos. Bless the grace. Bless the holy work of being a midlife woman with a full heart and an empty dishwasher.

You're doing better than you think.

Scripture Appendix

A collection of the verses featured throughout *Holy, Hormonal, and Holding On*

On Physical & Emotional Healing

- **Proverbs 14:30** – A heart at peace gives life to the body, but envy rots the bones.

- **John 5:6** – "Do you want to get well?"

- **Psalm 34:19** – Adonai is near to the brokenhearted and saves those crushed in spirit.

- **Isaiah 40:29** – He gives strength to the weary, and to one without vigor He adds might.

On Mental Clarity & Trust

- **1 Corinthians 14:33** – For God is not a God of confusion, but shalom.

- **Proverbs 3:5–6** – Trust in Adonai with all your heart... He will make your paths straight.

- **1 Thessalonians 5:24** – Faithful is the One who calls you—and He will make it happen!

On Comparison & Identity

- **Romans 13:13** – ...not in strife and envy.

- **James 3:16–17** – But the wisdom that is from above is... peaceable, gentle...

- **Galatians 6:4** – Each one must examine his own work...

On God's Timing & Purpose

- **2 Peter 3:9** – Adonai is not slow in keeping His promise...

- **Ecclesiastes 3:11** – He has made everything beautiful in its time.

- **Psalm 27:14** – Wait for Adonai. Be strong, let your heart take courage...

- **Romans 11:29** – The gifts and the calling of God are irrevocable.

On Relationships & Boundaries

- **Matthew 5:37** – But let your 'Yes' be 'Yes,' and your 'No' be 'No.'

- **Psalm 34:15** – Seek shalom and pursue it.

- **Romans 12:2** – Do not be conformed to this world...

- **Proverbs 12:26** – The righteous choose their friends carefully...

- **Proverbs 27:17** – Iron sharpens iron—so one person sharpens another.

On Marriage & Mercy

- **1 Peter 4:8** – Love covers a multitude of sins.

- **Ephesians 4:31–32** – Be kind to one another, compassionate, forgiving...

- **Ecclesiastes 4:9–10** – Two are better than one...

On Identity, Aging & Calling

- **Psalm 92:15** – Even in old age they will be fresh and flourishing.

- **Proverbs 20:29** – The splendor of old men is their gray hair.

- **Psalm 138:8** – Adonai will accomplish that which concerns me...

On Purpose, Legacy & Living Well

- **Proverbs 27:2** – Let another praise you, and not your own mouth...

- **Colossians 3:23** – Work at it from the soul, as for the Lord...

- **Proverbs 31:28–29** – Her children arise and bless her...

About the Author

Diane Ferreira is a Bible teacher, writer, and midlife cheerleader for every woman trying to keep her faith strong and her hormones in check.

She is the co-founder of *She Opens Her Bible™*, and *She's So Scripture™* on Substack: platforms designed to equip women with bold faith, biblical literacy, and a whole lot of joy.

A passionate student of Scripture, she holds a Graduate Certificate in Messianic Jewish Studies from MJTI and is currently pursuing her Master's in Jewish Studies.

Her work blends timeless biblical truth with a fresh, relatable voice that encourages women to laugh, cry, and lean into the goodness of God, even when life is messy.

Whether she's teaching, writing, or simply sharing her own "holy hot mess" journey, she brings heart, humor, and depth to everything she does.